No Two Zebras Look Exactly Alike

Stig Andersson

© Bokforlaget Libris, Orebro, Sweden
Printed in England 1979
by Purnell & Sons Ltd, Paulton (Bristol) and London
Coedition arranged with the help of Angus Hudson, London
ISBN 91-7194-170-3

American Edition
Chariot Books
David C. Cook Publishing Company
Elgin, IL 60120
ISBN: 0-89191-189-8

Peter and Lisa are brother and sister.

More than anything else, they like to go to the zoo together. It's always so much fun.

Something new and exciting is always going on there.

The last time they went to the zoo, there was a new little zebra there. It was only a few days old.

Uncle John, who takes care of the animals, said that it was all right for Lisa and Peter to pet the new zebra.

The two children would never have dared to pet the grown-up zebras. They seemed so wild and angry.

"Watch out for those wild, striped horses," Uncle John usually said.

But the little zebra was so cute! So warm and soft.

After awhile, the little zebra ran off in a straight line towards its mother.

"How did the little zebra know which one was his mother?" asked Peter. "All zebras look exactly alike."

Uncle John laughed and said, "The choice isn't so difficult for the little zebra. There are only eight zebras all together here at the zoo. But think about Africa, where the zebras live in huge flocks!"

"Think what would happen to the little zebra if he lost his mother in Africa. There are so many lions there," said Lisa.

"But how can he find his mother again, Uncle

John?" asked Peter. He worried about all the little lost zebras looking for their mothers.

"The mother and the little zebra recognize one another by the way they smell," said Uncle John. "When a baby zebra is looking for its mother, it sniffs at every zebra it meets. When he finally reaches his mother, he recognizes her by the way she smells.

"And look closely at the zebras we have here. You'll see that no two of them are exactly the same size. Their stripes are different, too."

The children did as Uncle John had told them, and sure enough, no two zebras were exactly alike!

Peter and Lisa gave all the zebras names. They called one Mr. Bigstripe and another Mrs. Littlestripe, and made up a lot of other funny-sounding names as well.

"You know, what's true about zebras is often true about people as well," said Uncle John. "Perhaps you think that people in some countries all look alike."

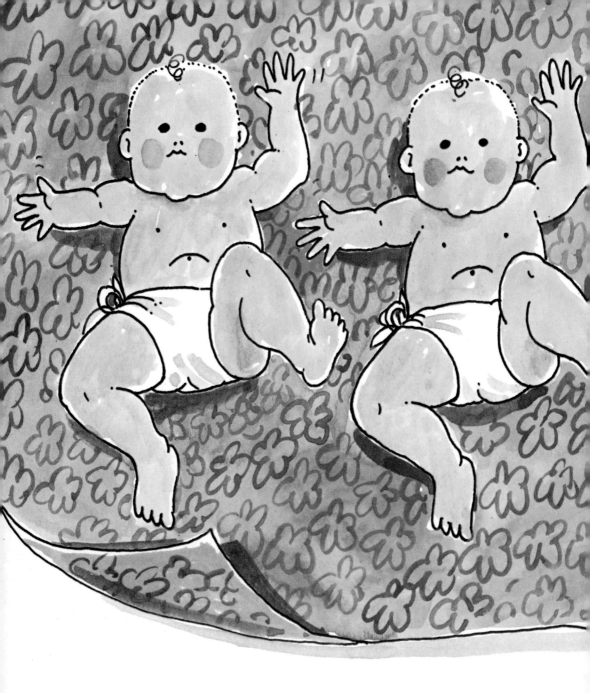

"If you see a lot of newborn babies all at once, they all look alike. But if you ask their mothers, you'll see that they know which baby is theirs at once."

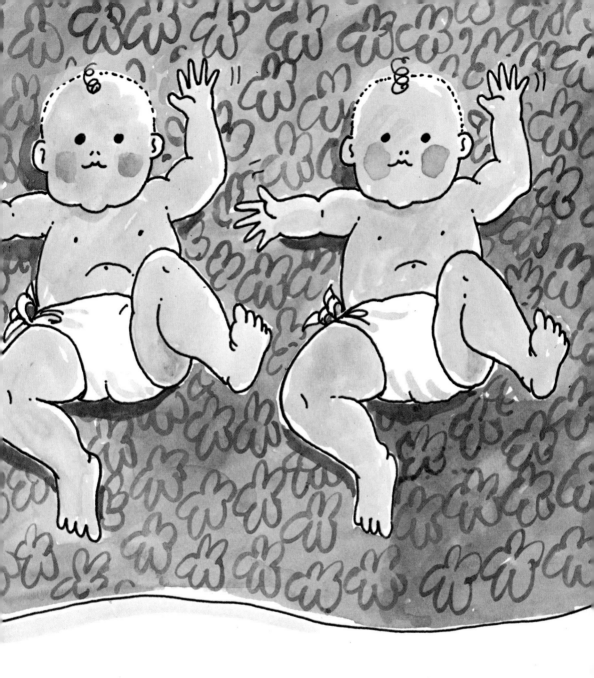

"One will say, 'Look what beautiful black hair my girl has.' Another will say, 'My little boy has his father's nose.' And so they go on. . ."

Children sometimes think that all grown-ups look alike. But they don't really look alike at all. There are tall ones and small ones, fat ones and thin ones. Some people have a pain in their back and have to walk with a stick.

There are people
with long, sharp
noses.

And others with round noses.

Some have no hair at all.

Others have a long, long beard.

Lisa spends a lot of time with four of her classmates. Their names are Jane, Karen, Anne, and Eve.

They play together all the time. But none of them looks like any of the others.

Jane is short and a little chubby. Karen is tall and thin. Anne was born in India. She has dark skin. Eve wears glasses and has freckles. Lisa has an upturned nose, and ears that she thinks are too big.

Peter has two good friends, Bobby and Paul. They're always getting into trouble together, but they're not at all alike. Bobby is strong and agile. He'll do just about anything you dare him to. Paul makes up the games they play,

en though he
metimes
oesn't dare to
the things
's dreamed up
mself. Peter is
ways on the
, and almost
ways dirty.

Bobby, Paul,
d Peter aren't
all alike, but
ey have a good
ne together
yway.

What if we *did* all look alike? What problems there would be!

What would happen if every girl in Lisa's class looked alike? Their teacher wouldn't know who she was talking to.

And what if all the teachers looked alike?

But that's not the way things are. . . .

God created us, the zebras and everything else.

And he made each of us different from everyone else.

All of us are important to God since he made us.

And he loves us, no matter what we look like.